American Police Work in English and Bidialectal Chinese

美國執法部門——英語及中文正簡對照版（英文、正體中文、簡體中文）

美国地方治安工作-英文及中文繁简对照版：（英文、繁体中文、简体中文）

Davis, Lai, Song

Rev. date: 10/10/2016

American Police Work in English and Bidialectal Chinese

美國執法部門——英語及中文正簡對照版（英文、正體中文、簡體中文）

美国地方治安工作-英文及中文繁简对照版：（英文、繁体中文、简体中文）

Authors, 作者，著者

Wayne L. Davis, Ph.D. （韋恩‧戴維斯 博士，

韋恩 L. 戴维斯博士 ）

Yu-Wen Lai （賴郁雯，赖郁雯)

Qiangjian Song （宋強建，宋强建)

Illustrators, 繪圖者，文中插画由 亚利亚纳．格里尔 提供

Brandon Lutterman, 布蘭登 •路特曼，布莱登．鲁特曼

Ariana Greer, 亞利安娜 •古雷爾， 亚里亚娜．格里尔

Derrick Freeman, 德瑞克 •費曼，德里克．弗里曼

Christian Connolly, 科里遜 •康諾利，克里斯蒂安．康纳利

Cover Photo: Yuan Peng, 封面照片 • 彭媛，

封面照片：彭媛

Table of Contents, 目錄, 目录

Declaration of Independence, 美國獨立宣言,

独立宣言 2

U.S. and State Constitutions, 美國憲法與州憲法,

美国宪法及各州宪法 4

U.S. Constitution, 美國憲法, 美国宪法 6

Academy and Continual Training, 警察學校及後續培訓,

警察学院及在职继续训练 8

City Police Officer, 城市警察, 市级警官 10

Sheriff, 縣治安官, 县治安官 12

Corrections Officer, 縣校軍官, 獄警 14

Bailiff, 法警，法警 16

State Trooper, 州警察，州际警官 18

Conservation Officers, 環保官員，保护区警官 20

Patrol Officers, 巡邏警察，巡警 22

Traffic Direction Cops, 交通指揮警察，交通警 24

Motorcycle Cops, 摩托車警察，摩托騎警 26

Mounted Police, 騎警，皇家騎警 28

Police Aviation – Helicopters, 航空警察——直升機，

航空警察－直升机 30

Police Aviation – Airplanes, 航空警察——飛機，

航空警察 －飞机 32

Bicycle Patrol, 自行車巡邏警察, 自行车巡逻警 34

Maritime Police, 海警, 海警 36

Canine Officer, 警犬警員, 警犬 38

Evidence Officer, 證據官, 证物处警官 40

Scuba Divers, 浮潛警員, 潜水警 42

Snowmobile Officers, 雪地車警員, 雪地警 44

School Resource Officers, 校園警察, 学校资源警官 ...46

Public Information Officers, 公關警察,

公共关系警官 48

SWAT Officers, 特種武器和戰術部隊, 特警 50

Bomb Squad Officer, 拆彈警察小組官員,

爆破专家 52

Defensive Tactics Instructor, 防守戰術指導員,

防御策略教官 54

Crash Investigators, 車禍調查警員,

车祸现场调查员 56

Crash Reconstructionist, 車禍復原警員,

车祸还原专家 58

Report Writing, 撰寫報告, 报告 60

Latent Fingerprints, 潛在指紋, 潜指印 62

Rolling Fingerprints, 按壓指紋，指紋取样 64

Interrogation, 審問，审讯 66

DNA (deoxyribonucleic acid) Analysis, DNA 分析，

DNA 分析 68

Search Crime Scenes, 搜尋犯罪現場，

搜索案发现场 70

School Presentations, 學校簡報，学校教学展示 72

Public Services, 公共服務，公共服务 74

Fire Control, 消防，消防 76

First Aid & CPR, 急救與心肺復甦，

心肺复苏急救 78

Police Officers are Compatriots,　警察是同胞,

警察是我们的同胞 ……….. 80

Preface

This book is designed for young readers. This book may be helpful to students who are learning multiple languages. This book presents information about U.S. local law enforcement work in English and bidialectal Chinese, which allow the students to make quick comparisons between the languages.

序

這本書專門設計給青少年朋友閱讀。本書對於學習多國語言的學生將有所助益。本書以三種不同語言（英文、正體中文、簡體中文）陳述美國警務工作的資訊，可使學生從中快速對照。

前言

本书的意向群体是年轻读者，特别是为那些正在学习多种语言又渴望了解美国公共安全的学生群体所作。因此，作者以三种不同的语言形式（英文、繁体中文、简体中文）将本书呈现给读者，旨在帮助读者从不同的文化视角进行比对、考量。

Declaration of Independence

According to the Declaration of Independence, the U.S. government derives its power from the people that it governs. Because there are more than 400 residents for every full-time police officer, social peace requires that people voluntarily comply with the law and assist with law enforcement efforts. Residents are stakeholders in maintaining a peaceful society and they must take an active part in promoting pro-social behaviors.

美國獨立宣言

根據美國獨立宣言，美國政府的權力來自其統治的人民。因為一名全職警察負責照顧超過四百個居民，社會安寧仰賴全民自發地遵守法律、協助法律執行成果。居民是對於維持和平社會之中有利害關係的人，他們必須積極提倡利社會行為，增進團體利益。

独立宣言

美国独立宣言确立了政府的权力来自其所服务的人民。美国的警民是四百比一，这意味每一位全职警官需要为四百位居民的人身安全和财产安全负责。由此可见，公共安全不仅仅是警察及相关机构的责任，它更需每一位居民以主人翁的精神来约束、规范自己的行为，并积极主动的参与、维护和帮助当地的执法机关以实现平安社会的目标。

U.S. and State Constitutions

The U.S. Constitution is the supreme law in America involving federal law. Until the U.S. Supreme Court makes a ruling, federal laws may be different in different federal jurisdictions. Each state also has its own state constitution. A state constitution is the supreme law within a state involving state law. Different states have different laws.

美國憲法與州憲法

美國憲法，包含聯邦法律，是在美國最有決定性的法律。直到最高法院裁決以前，聯邦法律在不同的聯邦管轄區域中可能會有所不同。每個州也有自己的州憲法。州憲法，包含州法律，是在所屬州裡具有最高決定權的法律。不同的州有不同的法律。

美国宪法及各州宪法

美国宪法是包含联邦法案的美国最高法律，因此美国的宪法高于一切法案。联邦法则因不同联邦法院的管辖权和司法权各有差异，而各州又有自己的州宪法。以此类推，各州的宪法是包含其州法案的最高法律，不同的州有着不同的法律。

4

U.S. Constitution

The U.S. Constitution requires that police follow the law. The U.S. Constitution protects people's privacy. However, the U.S. Constitution only provides civilians with minimum protection. The states may provide civilians with more protection against the government.

美國憲法

美國憲法要求警察守法。美國憲法保障人民的隱私。然而，美國憲法只提供市民最基本的保護。各州會提供更多保護市民不受政府欺負的法律。

美国宪法

美国宪法的执行需要其执法者首先是一个守法者。宪法保护人民的隐私。然而，宪法只能为人民群众提供最低限度的保护。而州宪法律则能为人民群众提供更多保护，以防联邦政府的过度管辖。

Academy and Continual Training

Police cadets must attend and pass a law enforcement academy before they can become police officers. Police cadets study law, they train to help and protect people, and they learn to drive a police car under stressful conditions. Even after graduating from the police academy, police officers must continually train.

警察學校及後續培訓

警校學員必須進入執法學院受訓，畢業以後，才能成為警察。警校學生學習法律，他們受訓的目標是為了幫助、保護人們，他們還要學會在充滿壓力的情況下駕駛警車。即使警察從警校畢業了，他們仍然要持續學習。

警察学院及继续训练

警察学员必须参加警察学院并通过最后考核才能成为一名正式的警官。警察学员需要学习法律，并被训练如何保护人民的安全，而且要学习能够在各种严峻的情况下，自如驾驶警车。甚至从警官学校毕业之后，警官仍需要参加各类在职继续训练。

City Police Officer

Here is a city police officer.

He is wearing a police uniform and a peaked cap.

He is wearing a badge on his uniform.

See the whistle chain leading to his right shirt pocket.

城市警察

他是一個城市警察。

他穿著警察制服，戴著有帽舌的帽子。

他的制服上別著徽章。

看看這個口哨鏈子掛在他的右側衣服上。

市级警官

这位是市级警官。

他身着警服并佩戴尖顶警帽。

他佩戴着警徽。

请看哨子链子连着警服上衣右边口袋。

11

Sheriff

Although the authority of a sheriff varies from jurisdiction to jurisdiction, the sheriff is an elected county official who is the chief law enforcement officer in any given county. A sheriff department oversees the county jail, provides security for courtrooms and judges, and delivers civil papers, such as jury summons and subpoenas.

縣治安官

　　儘管各個管轄區內的縣治安官的職責權力，差異很大，縣治安官是在所在郡內選舉獲選的官員，他是當地最主要的執法者。一個縣治安部門監督郡立監獄，保障審判室和法官的安全，傳遞民事訴狀，例如審判傳喚狀，以及傳票。

县治安官

　　县治安官的权限因执法区的不同有所变化，但是在其任职的县区内则是最高执法长官。一个县治安官所在的执法部门监督县级监狱、为法庭和法官提供安全保障，以及负责递送民事文件，比如：陪审团召集书和法庭传票。

Corrections Officer

Here is a county corrections officer.

She works for the sheriff department.

The sheriff, an elected official, runs the county jail.

She works inside the jail and watches inmates.

縣校軍官

她是一個縣校軍官。

她替縣治安官部門工作。

縣治安官是由選舉選出的官員，她負責管理該縣的監獄。

她在監獄裡工作，看管監獄犯人。

獄警

这是一位郡级狱警。

她在地方郡警局工作。

警长是由官方选立，负责本郡的监狱工作。

她在监狱工作，负责看守犯人。

Bailiff

A bailiff is a peace officer who provides court security. The bailiff ensures the safety of trial participants, provides assistance to judges, handles court documents, and enforces courtroom rules of behavior. The bailiff also announces the judge's entrance into the courtroom and provides jury escort outside of the courtroom to prevent jury contact with the public.

法警

法警保障法院的和平。法警確保參與審判者的安全、協助法官、處理法院文件、強制執行法庭行為規範。此外，法警的工作還包含宣佈法官進入法庭，以及在法庭外護送陪審團，避免陪審團與公眾接觸。

法警

法警是保障法庭安全的一种警种。法警的工作在于保证庭审出庭人员的安全、为法官提供辅助、处理庭审文件以及执行法庭行为要求。同时，法警也负责宣告法官的出席以及陪同陪审员出离法庭，以免陪审员与公众接触。

State Trooper

Here is a state trooper.

He is wearing a campaign hat.

He has a police radio microphone on his left shoulder.

州警察

這是一個州警察。

他戴一頂寬邊氈帽。

在他的左肩上，佩戴一個警察專用電台的麥克風。

州际警官

这是一位州际警官。

他佩戴的是一顶圆边礼帽。

在他的左肩上配有警用对讲机。

Conservation Officers

A conservation officer is sometimes called a game warden. A conservation officer is a police officer who protects wildlife and the environment. They protect game, catch poachers, and protect streams from being polluted. They also make sure that people enjoy the wilderness in a safe manner.

環保官員

環保官員有時也稱作「野生動物保護區管理員」。環保官員是保護野生動物和環境的警察。他們保護動物、抓盜獵者，避免溪流被污染。他們也保障人民可以安全地享受大自然環境。

保护区警官

保护区警官有时又被称为渔猎警官，他们的职责在于保护野生动物和自然环境。保护区警官保护狩猎活动、防范盗猎者并保护河流免受污染，同时又保障人们在合法合理的条件下享受自然及野生资源。

Patrol Officers

Some police officers ride around in police cars. The officers keep an eye out for crime and traffic violations. Officers listen to many different radios, including the high frequency police radio, the low frequency police radio, and the CB radio. The dispatcher at the post will use a police radio, computer, or phone to inform the officer of a work detail and where to go. A work detail may include diffusing a volatile situation, interviewing a witness, protecting a hazardous scene, or recovering found items.

巡邏警察

有些警察坐在警車裡四處巡視。這些巡邏警察搜尋犯罪和交通違規。警員會聽許多不同的廣播電台，包含高頻率警察電台、低頻率警察電台，與民用波段電台（Citizen Band Radio）。負責發送公告的派遣員會使用警用電台、電腦、電話，通知警員工作上的細節以及要到哪裡去。工作上的細節包含通知違規情況、面談目擊證人、保護危險的犯罪現場，或復原找到的物件。

巡警

有一种警种是驾驶警车的巡逻警。他们的职责在于提防罪案及监督违反公共交通的行为。巡警时常收听收音机，包括高频率和低频率的警察无线电，以及一些民用波段。警察总部会使用无线电、电脑、电话通知执勤巡警任务细节和任务目的地。任务细节有可能包括在具有危险性的情况下疏散人群、访问目击者、保护案发现场或者是寻找重要证物。

Traffic Direction Cops

Some police officers stand on busy street corners and direct traffic. The officers may use whistles, flashlights, and reflective traffic sticks to control the movement of cars. After the traffic in a particular direction has been stopped, the officers will allow people to safely walk across the street. These police officers work in rain, sleet, snow, and extreme heat.

交通指揮警察

有些警察站在忙碌的街頭角落，指揮交通。交通警察會使用哨子、手電筒、反光指揮棒來控制車流。在某一個方向的車子都停下來以後，警察會讓行人安全地過馬路。這些交通警察在雨中、雪中、雨雪交加，或是極炎熱的天氣下工作。

交通警察

有一种警种是站立在繁闹的街区和街角指挥交通的交通警察，简称"交警"。交警往往会使用哨子、手电筒和交通反光棒来指挥交通。在指挥制停某个方向的车辆后，交警会示意行人安全地穿过街道。无论刮风下雨、严寒酷暑，交警都尽职尽责地出现在指挥交通的第一线。

Motorcycle Cops

Some police officers ride motorcycles. Motorcycles are more maneuverable than police cars, which may be advantageous on crowded streets. A motorcycle's relatively small size allows it to get to a crash scene more quickly than a police car when traffic is congested. Because motorcycles are smaller and lighter than cars, they are more fuel and cost efficient. Officers who ride motorcycles focus on traffic violations. They stop cars for going too fast, following too close, and disregarding traffic signals. The officers may write these drivers tickets.

摩托車警察

有些警察騎摩托車。摩托車比起警用汽車更好操控，而且在擁擠的道路上更佔優勢。與汽車相比，摩托車相對較小的體積，可以讓警察在塞車時更快到達車禍現場，而且節省汽油支出。摩托車警察專門處理交通違規。他們會擋下行進速度過快的、跟車跟得太近的、違反交通號誌的車輛。這些警員能開不守秩序的駕駛罰單。

摩托骑警

有一种警种是骑摩托车出勤的摩托骑警。与警车相比，摩托车更具便捷性，尤其在人群拥挤的街区。摩托车的优势体现在能更迅捷地到达车祸现场，而警车则受制于当时的交通情况。因为摩托车轻巧的特性，使得它更经济实惠。骑警的职责在于维持交通安全，他们会制止那些超速的车辆、车距过近的车辆以及那些无视交通指示灯的车辆。通常，摩托骑警会对违反交通者出示罚单。

Mounted Police

In some areas, police officers ride horses. In some jurisdictions, horses are considered vehicles. Police officers who ride horses are called mounted police. Horses can carry police officers where cars and motorcycles cannot go, such as in parks and in rough terrain areas. This may be essential for search and rescue efforts. Horses give police officers added height and visibility. The weight of a horse allows police officers to disperse unruly crowds.

騎警

在某些地區的警察需要騎馬。在有些管轄區域裡，馬匹算是車輛的一種。騎著馬的警察被稱作騎警。馬兒可以帶警察到一些汽車與摩托車不能到的地方，例如公園和崎嶇的地帶。這對於搜救尤其重要。馬兒可以增加警察的高度，讓警察有更好的視野。馬兒的重量可讓警察驅散難以控制的群眾。

皇家骑警

有一种警种是骑马出勤的警官。在某些治安管辖区，马被视为交通工具，皇家骑警便由此得名。骑马的优势是在于，马匹能够在警车和摩托车都无法抵达的情况下将警官送达目的地。例如，公园和一些地形崎岖的山地。这对于一些特殊的搜救行动至关重要。骑马的另一优势在于能够给予警官格外的高度和视角，并且马匹的重量可以警官更容易地驱散那些不与合作的人群。

Police Aviation – Helicopters

Some police officers fly in helicopters. A helicopter has wings that rotate. Helicopters can hover and they can land in tight spaces. Police officers in helicopters watch for traffic jams and crashes on busy roadways. Helicopters have infrared, which allows the officers to see objects in the dark.

航空警察——直升機

有些警察駕駛直升機。直升機有旋轉的機翼。直升機可以在空中盤旋，而且能降落在較小的空間。航空警察坐在直升機裡，觀察擁塞交通和繁忙道路的車禍。直升機配有紅外線，能讓警察在黑暗中看得清楚。

航空警察－直升机

有一种警种是驾驶直升机出勤的航空警察。直升机的机翼是活动的，可以旋转。随着机翼盘旋将机身带至空中，同时又可以在相对狭小的场地降落。通过直升机，航空警察可以在拥挤的路段观察车祸现场。直升机自带的红外线可以帮助航空警察在夜里锁定目标。

Police Aviation - Airplanes

Some police officers fly in airplanes. An airplane has fixed wings that do not rotate. Compared to helicopters, airplanes can travel faster, farther, higher, and can be operated at a much lower cost. An airplane can be used to clock a vehicle's speed on the roadway by seeing how long it takes for the car to travel between two fixed points (speed = distance / time).

航空警察——飛機

有些警察駕駛飛機。飛機有固定的機翼，機翼不會旋轉。與直升機相比，飛機飛得更快、更遠、更高，而且操作的花費比較低。藉著觀察汽車通過兩個定點之間需花費多長時間，一架飛機可以測量路面車輛的速度。

航空警察—飞机

也有一些警官是乘坐大型飞机出勤执行任务。飞机的机翼是固定的，无法旋转。相比直升机，飞机可以航行的更快、更远、更高，并且乘坐飞机执行任务的成本远低于直升机。利用飞机的高空作业性能，通过计算始发地和目的地的距离及时间，执勤人员能够轻易计算出一辆交通工具的速度（速度＝距离／时间）。

Bicycle Patrol

Some police officers ride on bicycles. Bike officers can travel faster and farther than foot patrol officers, they are able to patrol areas unreachable by car, they have a stealth advantage because they are silent, and they are cost effective. Bike patrol is very effective during special events, such as parades. Bicycles allow officers to better interact with the public, which is important for developing relationships. Police-community relationships are essential because community members have important knowledge that is essential for finding solutions to local problems.

自行車巡邏警察

有些警察騎自行車。比起徒步巡邏的警察，自行車巡警移動速度較快，也可以到達較遠的地方，他們能在一些汽車到不了的地方巡邏。由於騎自行車很安靜，所以佔有隱秘的優勢，在開銷方面也比較省錢。在特別的場合下，例如遊行，騎自行車巡邏很有效率。自行車巡邏可讓警察更容易與公眾互動，是警察發展社區關係的重要環節。

自行车巡逻警

有一种警种是骑自行车出行执勤的。自行车巡逻警能够更快、更远地到达那些警车无法达到的地区。自行车轻巧无声，使其极具隐蔽性并且投入成本很低。自行车巡逻在某些特殊的情形下非常有效，游行就是一个很好的例子。骑自行车巡逻能够帮助警官和大众更好的交流互动，这对于培养公共关系至关重要。警官和社区的公共关系之所以关键在于大多数的社区群众具有重要的知识能够帮助解决当地的问题。

Maritime Police

Maritime police officers patrol in watercraft. Their patrol areas may be coastal canals, rivers, lakes, harbors, and/or sea waters. They can reach locations not easily accessible by land. Maritime police officers promote the safety of water users by enforcing laws related to water traffic. Maritime police guard things on the dock, protect maritime animals, and prevent smuggling.

海警

海警開船巡邏。他們巡邏的區域包含沿海運河、河流、湖、港口、（或）海。他們能去一些從陸地不容易到達的地方。海警執行涉及海上交通的法律，藉此促進海上使用者的安全。海警保衛碼頭上的物品，保護海洋動物，並預防走私。

海警

有一种警种是驾驶水上交通工具出勤的海警。他们的执勤范围可能是海洋、运河、河流、湖泊、港口。海警的优势在于，他们可以到达陆地无法触及的区域。通过执行海域相关法令，海警保证了航海安全和海域安全。同时，海警的职责还包括保证海港船只的安全，并防范走私等非法活动。

Canine Officer

Canine (K-9) officers go to a special school and learn how to work with dogs. Canines (dogs) have a much better sense of smell than do humans. Officers use their dogs to search for drugs, accelerants, explosives, cadavers, evidence, and missing people. Police officers and their dogs become very close and they work together as a team. The police dog is considered a police officer.

警犬警員

警犬（英文 canine 的諧音：K-9）警員去專門學校學習如何與狗一起工作。狗的嗅覺比起人類靈敏許多。警員會利用狗來搜尋毒品、燃燒促進劑、炸藥、屍體、證物，和失蹤人口。警員與他們的警犬關係緊密，而且他們在同個團隊工作。警犬被視為警察的一員。

警犬

帶犬警官（k-9）在特殊的学校受训学习如何与警犬合作。警犬的嗅觉比人类更灵敏。帶犬警官会使用警犬搜寻毒品、促进剂、爆炸物、尸体、证物以及失踪人口。通常，警官会他们的警犬关系密切，团队协作。警犬同样被认为是一名警员。

Evidence Officer

The evidence officer is responsible for the intake, storage, and disposal of all property collected by the department. The officer ensures that evidence is secure from theft, loss, and contamination. The officer transports property to the crime lab, maintains chain of custody reports, notifies property owners when they can get their property back, and coordinates the court-ordered disposal of contraband.

證據官

證據官負責納入、儲存、丟棄所有部門搜集來的證物。證據官確保證物免於偷竊、遺失和污染。證據官運送證物到犯罪實驗室，維持保管記錄的正確性，通知證物持有者何時可以拿回他們的物品，以及協調法院明令需丟棄的走私物。

证物室警官

证物室警官的职责是接收、储存并处理一切警务部门的一切重要物件。证物室警官要防止证物被盗窃、丢失和被污染。证物室警官的职责是：将证物送至犯罪实验室、处理受保管证物报告，在恰当的时候知会主人领取证物，并协调处理法庭指定的赃品。

Scuba Divers

Some police officer are scuba divers. They are specially trained in underwater rescue, underwater recovery, and underwater investigation. Scuba divers carry their own source of air on their back, which allows them to breathe underwater. Police divers might need to dive in murky, dark, cold water with strong currents and parasites. Scuba divers must be able to swim.

浮潛警員

有些警察是浮潛員。他們接受海底救援、修復、調查的特訓。浮潛警員背著氧氣筒，這可使他們在海裡呼吸。浮潛警員有可能必須潛入污濁、黑暗、冰冷，且帶有潮流和寄生蟲的水裡。浮潛警員必須會游泳。

潜水警

有一种警种是潜水警。他们受训水下搜救、水下维修以及水下侦查。潜水员会背着一个氧气筒，使他们可以在水下安全作业。潜水警可能需要潜入阴暗冰冷、充满寄生虫和带有电流的水域。当然，潜水警一定要会游泳。

Snowmobile Officers

Snowmobiles allow police officers to respond to emergencies in snow storms. During blizzards, cars may get stuck on the roadway. The snow becomes too deep and the roadway becomes very slippery. Snowmobiles allow police officers to travel along impassable roadways in order to aid stranded motorists. Snowmobiles also allow police officers to travel off road and onto ice-covered lakes.

雪地車警員

雪地車可讓警察在暴風雪時，針對急難狀況做出回應。暴風雪時，車子可能會困在路上。雪積得更深，而道路變得更滑。雪地車能讓警察穿越無法通行的道路，救援受困的駕駛人。雪地車也能帶警察到沒有柏油路的地方，甚至是冰雪覆蓋的湖面上。

雪地警

雪地车帮助警官们在大雪风暴时仍能出勤紧急情况。在暴风雪天气，因雪太厚、地太滑，警车常常会抛锚在路上。在种情况下，雪地车则可以畅行无阻，能够及时帮助受困司机脱险。不仅如此，雪地车还能帮助警官们出离地面，在冰冻的湖面上行驶。

School Resource Officers

Some police departments assign police officers to work within public schools. These police officers are called school resource officers. School resource officers are responsible for providing security and crime prevention services within the educational environment. The school resource officer has three main responsibilities: teacher, counselor, and law enforcement officer.

校園警察

有些警察局會指派警察到公立學校。這些警察稱為駐校警察。駐校警察負責校園安全以及預防犯罪駐校警察身兼三項責任：老師、咨詢員、及執法人員。

学校资源警官

某些警察部门会指派警官与一些公共学校合作。这类警官被称为学校资源警官。该警种的警官会负责教育环境的公共安全和罪案预防。他们身兼数职：教师、咨询顾问和执法者。

47

Public Information Officers

The police department's professional reputation and the public's support depend on good police-media relations. The police are accountable to the public and the media are the community watchdogs. When a crisis event occurs, the police must have a trained public relations officer readily available to communicate with the media. The police need to monitor the messages that the media deliver to the public.

公關警察

警察局的聲譽和民眾支持度，有賴於警察與媒體之間的良好關係。警察對公眾負責，而媒體是社區的監察人。緊急事件發生時，一定會有專門負責公共關係的警察與媒體溝通。警察必須監控媒體傳達給大眾的訊息。

公共关系警官

警察部门的形象和影响力取决于与媒体之间的关系。当警察部门为社区公共安全负责的时候，媒体则是社区的守护者。因此，当突发状况发生时，警察部门需要有训练有素的警官负责与媒体沟通。警察部门亦须监督媒体向大众释放的信息。

SWAT Officers

Some police departments may have a special weapons and tactics (SWAT) team. SWAT officers are specially trained to intervene in high-risk and dangerous situations. When patrol officers are overwhelmed and need emergency help, the SWAT team may be called to assist.

特種武器和戰術部隊

某些警察局會有特種武器和戰術部隊，簡稱 SWAT 特種警察部隊。特種警察部隊受過特訓，專門處理高風險、危險的任務。當巡邏警察忙不過來，需要緊急協助時，特種警察部隊會被請來幫忙。

特警

某些警察部门会有一支训练有素的特殊警种，简称特种警察（SWAT）。特警特别为高危的突发状况而受训。当巡警在难以招架一些突发状况的时候，通常会依赖于特警的帮助。

51

Bomb Squad Officer

A bomb squad officer is trained to find, approach, handle, and neutralize packages that may contain powerful explosives. A bomb squad officer will don a special bomb suit that will protect the officer from a blast. Tools used by bomb squad officers may include robots, mirrors, canines, x-ray devices, disrupter guns, laser scopes, bomb baskets, bomb cylinders, and special bomb trucks.

拆彈警察小組官員

拆彈警組官員受過專門訓練，他們尋找、接近、處理、摧毀可能含有強大炸藥的包裹。拆彈警組官員會穿特殊的防彈衣，以保護他們免於炸彈衝擊。他們使用的工具包含機器人、鏡子、警犬、X射線裝置、拆彈用水波槍、雷射檢測鏡、防爆罐、彈筒，與專門放炸彈的卡車。

爆破专家

爆破专家是受训去搜索、接近、处理以及销毁那些带有强烈爆炸物的包裹的警官。爆破专家会穿着专门的防爆服，以防爆炸危害。他们使用的辅助工具有：机器人、镜子、警犬、x光设备、爆破枪、激光显示器、爆破桶、爆破汽缸和特殊的防爆卡车。

Defensive Tactics Instructor

In the U.S., there are rules for the type and amount of force that police officers can legally use against offenders to overcome resistance. A defensive tactics instructor is a certified officer who trains police officers in the proper use of force. In addition to their hands and feet, tools used by defensive tactics instructors include striking pads, handcuffs, batons, pepper spray, and training guns.

防守戰術指導員

在美國，警察可合法用來對抗侵犯者的武力，針對這種防禦，有種類和數量的規範。防守戰術指導員是通過認證的警員，負責訓練警察使用適當的武力。除了使用他們的手腳以外，防守戰術指導員還會使用拳擊擋板、手銬、指揮棒、胡椒噴霧，以及訓練用槍。

防御策略教官

在美国警察合法地实用暴力去制止抗法行为的类型和数量是有严格规定的。防御策略教官是经专业核准去训练警官合法实用暴力的专家。除手脚外，防御策略教官还有一些常备工具：拳靶、手铐、警棍、胡椒喷雾剂和训练枪。

Crash Investigators

Police officers investigate vehicle crashes. Police officers want to know why each crash happened. An officer will use a measuring wheel to measure distances and a protractor or compass to measure angles. It is not always possible to measure all the distances and angles due to the terrain. However, math can be used to calculate the missing variables. A drag sled can be used to measure road surface friction. With this information, the speed and direction of the vehicles can be calculated prior to the collision.

車禍調查警員

警察調查車禍。他們希望知道每場車禍發生的原因。警察會使用測量輪和量角器或指南針來測量角度。依據不同地帶，並不是每次都能測量所有的距離和角度。但是，數學可用來計算遺失的變量。拖動雪橇可用來測量路面的摩擦。有了這項資訊，車輛的速度及方向就可在擦撞前被計算出來。

车祸现场调查员

警察的另一职责是调查车祸情况。为了知道是什么因素导致了车祸的发生，警方会通过计量轮和圆规，根据地形来测量距离和角度。不过，在这里数学可以很好地用来计算那些未被纳入考虑的变量。同时，托橇可以用来检测路面摩擦情况。通过各类技术获得的信息可以帮助警方了解在车祸发生前车辆行驶的速度。

Crash Reconstructionist

A crash reconstructionist is a police officer who has received specialized training to investigate serious vehicle crashes. The officer will use scientific processes to identify the causes of a crash by considering the vehicle design, vehicle damage, speed of operation, lamp filaments, yaw marks, the roadway, and the environment. Officers use mathematics and physics to determine fault and to assign blame.

事故現場重建警員

事故現場重建警員是受過特訓，專門調查嚴重車禍的警察。事故現場重建警員使用科學方法，諸如考量汽車的造型設計、汽車的損傷、駕駛車速、燈絲、偏航輪胎軌跡、道路及整體環境狀況等，以鑑識車禍發生的原因。事故現場重建警員也利用數學和物理來釐清責任歸屬，判定誰對誰錯。

车祸还原专家

车祸事故还原专家是一种经过特殊训练的警官，主要任务在于调查严重的车祸事故。警官使用科学的方法，将车辆设计、车辆受损程度、行驶速度、灯丝、车胎拖痕、路况以及现场环境等因素纳入考量，用以断定事故原因。警官们会利用数学和物理来确认正误并决定事故责任人。

Report Writing

Police officers write many different types of reports. Some of the reports include affidavits, crash reports, public service reports, intelligence reports, and case reports. Criminal reports are based on the elements of the law. English and math are required to properly interpret the law. Improper grammar will impact the truth value or meaning of the law. Police officers must use English and math to effectively write reports.

撰寫報告

警察撰寫各式各樣的報告。這些報告包含口供、車禍記錄、公共服務記錄、情報、案例報告。犯罪報告是基於「犯罪的要素」（證明被告者有罪的事實）。他們需要使用正確的英文和數學詮釋法律。不恰當的文法會影響事實的正確性或法律的意思。警察必須善用英文和數學來有效率地撰寫報告。

报告

警官通常需要写各类不同的报告。报告范围包括：宣誓书、车祸报告、公共服务报告、智力报告、案件报告。罪案报告是根据法律的要素参照、比对来完成，并要求对语义的解读和用数学的分析来诠释法律。语法的误差往往会对法律解读的真确性造成影响。警官们必须用英文和数学有效地完成报告。

Latent Fingerprints

All fingerprints are unique. Once a fingerprint is collected, it can be used to identify the person who left it behind. Latent fingerprints are fingerprints left at a crime scene that may not be immediately visible to the naked eye. Police officers use magnetic and nonmagnetic colored powders to find the invisible fingerprints. Other techniques to find invisible fingerprints include superglue fumes and chemical sprays.

潛在指紋

所有的指紋都是獨一無二的。一旦指紋被探集， 它就可以用來識別是哪個人留下的。潛在指紋是在犯罪現場裡無法立即被肉眼察覺出來的指紋。警察使用磁性和非磁性彩色粉末來找到肉眼看不見的指紋。我們還可以利用強力膠煙霧和化學噴霧， 找到看不見的指紋。

潜指印

每一个指纹都是独一无二的。任何一个指纹都能够帮助警官确定它的主人是谁。"潜指印"是指那些留在犯罪现场的， 无法立刻用肉眼看到的指纹。警官们用有色带有磁性的粉末和有色没有磁性的粉末来找到那些我们无法用肉眼观察的指纹。其他的用来找到无法用肉眼观察的潜指印的技术有：强力胶喷雾和化学喷雾。

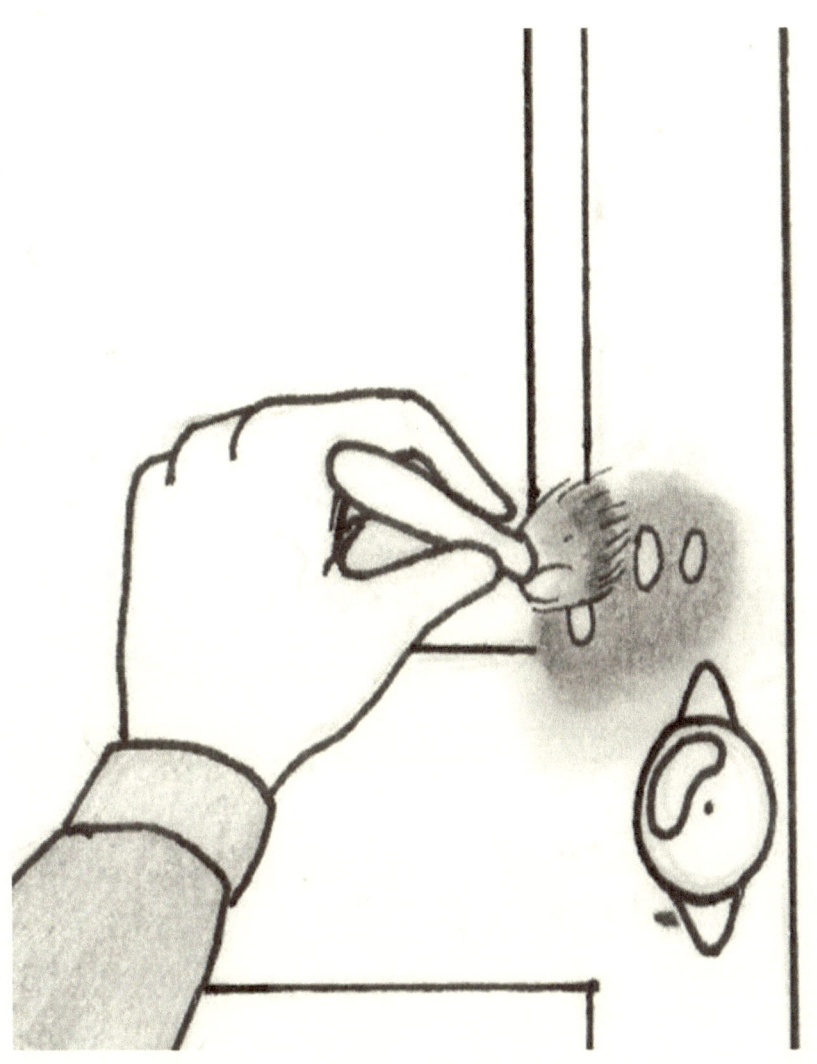

Rolling Fingerprints

Once an adult has been arrested by the police, a corrections officer will need to book the defendant into the jail. In order to properly identify the accused, a law enforcer will take the suspect's fingerprints. The officer will place each of the suspect's fingers into black ink and will then roll each finger onto a red fingerprint card. Some departments can perform this task electronically without ink. A blue fingerprint card is used for background checks and are not used for criminal purposes.

按壓指紋

一旦一名成年人被警察逮捕，縣校軍官將會送這個罪犯入獄。為了妥善辨別這個罪犯的身份，執法人員會採集這名嫌疑犯的指紋。警察會將嫌犯的指紋放入黑色墨水，然後按壓每個指頭到一張紅色的指紋卡上。有些部門利用電子設備按壓指紋，而不需要墨水。藍色的指紋卡用於身家背景調查，而不適用於犯罪者。

指纹取样

当警察抓获一个成年人之后，狱警需要将嫌疑犯送到监狱去。将疑犯的指纹取样，能够帮助警官们确定该 疑犯的身份。所以，警官会将疑犯的手指沾上黑墨水，然后按压犯人手指，将疑犯的指纹印在红色指纹卡上。有些部门已经通过全程电子化作业，无需使用墨水。需注意：蓝色指纹是用于背景调查，而非犯罪调查的用途。

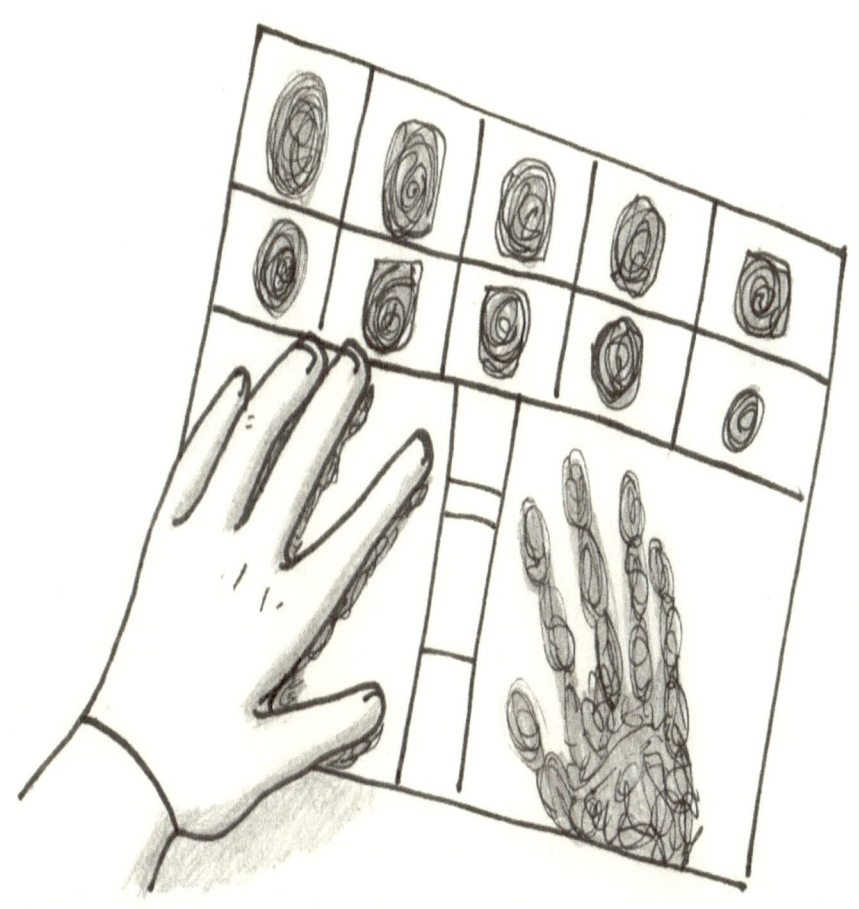

Interrogation

The police only need to be 51% confident that a crime occurred in order to make an arrest. Interrogation exists when a person is under arrest and is being questioned by police about the commission of a specific crime. When being interrogated, the person has a right to a lawyer and may stop answering questions at any time.

審問

警察只要有51%的信心認定犯罪事件發生，就可以成立逮捕行動。審問就是當嫌疑犯遭到逮捕，被警察問訊是不是犯下特定罪行。嫌疑犯被審問時，他有權利申請律師陪同，並且能夠隨時拒絕回答問題。

审讯

在罪案发生时，警察只需要51%的确信就可以实行抓捕。审讯，是当某人因为某项具体的犯罪案件而被捕时，接受警察的质询和审问。在被审讯时，此人有权力申请律师，并且因此可以在任何时候拒绝回答问题。

DNA (deoxyribonucleic acid) Analysis

Police officers may need to collect DNA evidence at a crime scene. DNA is a person's genetic blueprint that can be used for identification purposes. A person's bodily fluids, such as blood, contain DNA evidence. Blood can be collected via cotton swabs and placed into a cardboard box. Blood should not be placed into a plastic bag because it will putrefy and become ruined. Properly collected blood evidence can then be sent to the crime lab for DNA analysis. To maintain the integrity of the evidence, the police will seal the box and will use a chain of custody form to indicate all persons who have handled the evidence.

DNA （去氧核糖核酸）分析

警察有時需要在犯罪現場搜集 DNA 證據。DNA 是一個人的基因藍圖，可以用來鑑定身份。人類的體液，例如血液，含有 DNA。血液能透過棉花棒採集，放到硬紙箱裡。血液不該放進塑膠袋，因為它會在很短的時間內腐壞。利用適當方式搜集的血液會被送去犯罪實驗室進行 DNA 分析。為了維持證物完整性，警察會密封箱子，並使用一連串的保管表格，記錄有哪些人員經手過這個箱子。

DNA (脱氧核糖核苷酸)分析

警察可能需要在犯罪现场收集 DNA 证据。DNA 是一个人的基因密码，用以确认身份。一个人的体液，比如血液，就含有 DNA 证据。血液可以通过棉纱布收集，然后放置于纸盒内。切忌将血液样本放置于塑料袋中，因为塑料会导致血液样本在很短的时间内变质、腐化。合宜地将血液取样，随后即可送至罪案实验室用以 DNA 分析。为了确保证物的完整性，警方通常会将该置物盒密封并用监管链示意所有处理相关证物的人员。

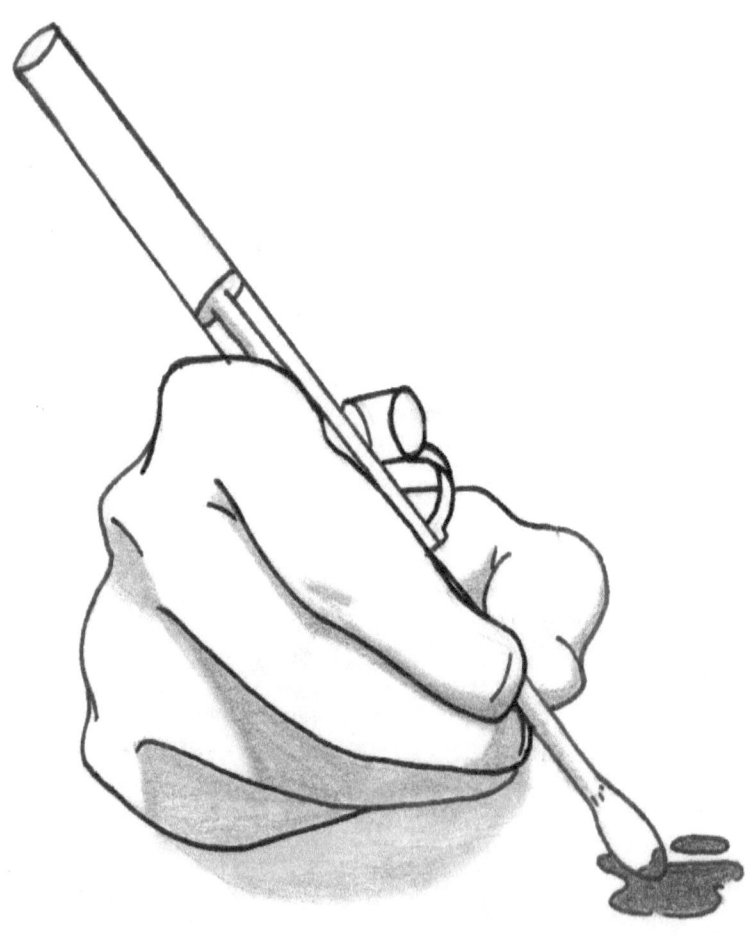

Search Crime Scenes

Police officers search areas for lost people and items. The police need to have a plan of action in order to cover the area most efficiently and effectively. Different search techniques should be used for different purposes and different locations. Sometimes the police need to find a person in an unknown direction. Other times the police need to find a small item in a known area.

搜尋犯罪現場

警察搜尋不同區域的失蹤人口與物品。警察需要行動計劃，好讓搜尋涵蓋區域更有效率。在不同的目的與區域，應該使用不同的搜尋技巧。有時候警察需要從一個未知的方向找一個人，有時警察需要在一個已知的地區找尋一個小物品。

搜索罪案现场

警方会在不同的区域搜索失踪人口和相关证物。通常，在搜索行动开展前，警方会进行缜密的计划部署以便更有效地、更迅捷地覆盖所要搜索的区域。特殊情况，特殊处理。所以，搜索策略和相关技术会随案件情况、区域地形和搜索目标的不同有所差异。常常警方需要在不清楚具体方向的情况下寻找某个相关人员。有时，警方需要在已知区域寻找某个极小的证物。

School Presentations

Knowledge is a valuable tool. Police officers attempt to educate students to promote safety and health. Police officers may show videos and pass out brochures. Police officers may also let students wear inebriation goggles so that they can experience the disorientation effects caused by alcohol and drugs. The intoxication goggles are safe, fun to use, and do not cause drunkenness.

學校簡報

知識是寶貴的工具。警察試圖教育學生以提倡安全與健康意識。警察會播放影片和發送宣傳手冊。警察有時也會讓學生試戴「醉酒眼鏡」，好讓他們體驗酒精和毒品帶來的迷失方向感。醉酒眼鏡使用上安全、有趣，且不會造成醉酒。

学校教学展示

知识是极具价值的一种工具。因此，警官常常会进入校园，通过对学生的教育来促进健康、安全等相关知识。常见的方法有：播放视频和分发须知手册。有时，警官们会让同学们佩戴模拟眼镜，以感受酒醉后或吸毒后的状态。当然，这种模拟眼镜是安全的，甚至很有娱乐性，并不会产生任何醉酒或吸毒相关的副作用。

Public Services

Police officers promote traffic safety and perform public services. When a car on the road gets a flat tire, a police officer can change the tire for the driver. Because it is unsafe for an occupied car to be parked on the berm, changing the tire helps fix the car so that it can be moved out of harm's way.

公共服務

警察提倡交通安全，執行公共服務。當一輛行駛中的車爆胎了，警察會幫駕駛換輪胎。因為停靠在路肩的車是不安全的，警察幫忙換輪胎可以讓車子早點移開路肩。

公共服务

警察除了要保证交通安全，还需要提供公共服务。比如，当一辆汽车因为轮胎瘪了而抛锚时，警官可以帮助司机更换轮胎。将一辆搭载乘客的汽车停靠的路肩是非常危险的，因此帮助司机及时更换轮胎并将汽车驶离可大大降低伤亡和损失。

Fire Control

Some police officers are public safety officers who are trained in fire suppression. Police officers will use fire extinguishers to control fires. Police officers must use the right kind of fire extinguisher for each specific type of fire. For example, a water type fire extinguisher is appropriate for wood fires but is extremely dangerous for cooking oil fires. A carbon dioxide fire extinguisher is effective for cooking oil fires, but it does not work well for wood fires. Smoke from fires can be extremely hot and poisonous.

消防

有些警察負責公共安全，他們的職責是滅火。警察用滅火器控制火勢。警察一定要使用正確的滅火器以應對不同形式的火災。舉例來說，噴水式的滅火器適用於木材引起的火勢，但對於食用油導致的火災則非常危險。二氧化碳滅火器對於食用油導致的火災很有用，但對於木材引起的火勢則沒有幫助。火災產生的煙非常熱，而且具有毒性。

消防

有一种警察是负责公共安全的警种，他们受过灭火训练。警官们会使用灭火器来控制火情，而因火种的不同，警官需要熟悉了解具体使用哪种灭火器。比如，对于森林或木制品相关的火情，显然使用水管喷水灭火是非常适合的；然而，同样的方法对于厨房因食用油所导致的火情则非常危险。这个时候，干冰便是最适合用来熄灭这类火情的灭火器。相反，干冰对于森林或木制品的火情完全不适用。大火导致的浓烟热度非常高，并含有剧毒。

First Aid & CPR

Sometimes people need immediate medical assistance when no doctors are readily available. Police officers are trained in first aid and cardiopulmonary resuscitation (CPR). The American Red Cross offers first aid training. The ABCs of first aid are Airway, Breathing, and Circulation. Police officer are trained to use Automated External Defibrillators, a portable device that checks the heart rhythm and sends an electric shock to the heart, when needed, in an attempt to restore a normal rhythm. First aid includes simple procedures such as dressing a wound, setting a bone with a splint, treating a burn with ointment, and stopping blood loss by applying pressure. The goal is to preserve life, to prevent further harm, and to promote recovery.

急救與心肺復甦

在沒有醫生能馬上救援的情況，有時候人們需要即刻的醫療協助。警察受過由美國紅十字會提供的心肺復甦的訓練。最基礎的急救是 ABCs，A 就是 Airway （保持呼吸道暢通），B 就是 Breathing （人工呼吸），C 就是 Circulation （胸部按壓）。警察受過「自動體外心臟去顫器」的使用訓練。自動體外心臟去顫器是一種攜帶型裝置，可檢測心律，並在試圖維持心臟正常的律動時，發送電擊到心臟。急救包含了簡單的程序，例如包紮傷口、將骨頭用夾板固定、在燙傷處敷上藥膏、施壓止血以避免血液流失等。目的是保護生命、預防更嚴重的傷口，以及促進恢復速度。

心肺复苏急救

有时人们常常会遇到一些突发的药疗状况，却没有医生在场。因此，警官们接受心肺复苏急救训练是十分必要。美国红十字会在这方面协助提供急救护理训练项目。急救护理的三要素是：通风、呼吸和血液流通。警官们受训学会使用自动体外心脏去颤器，顾名思义，这是能监测心脏起搏状况，并在必要的情况下通过电流刺激心脏以使其规律化的一种机器。基础的急救护理包括：包扎伤口、给断骨上夹板、用药膏涂抹烧伤、按压伤口防治失血过多。最终目标是维持生命、防止情况恶化以及促进恢复。

Police Officers Are Compatriots

Police officers are part of the local community. They are compatriots who have a vested interest in developing and maintaining a peaceful society. They have families and friends like everyone else. Police officers are peacemakers who have sworn to serve the public.

警察是同胞

警察是當地社區的一份子。在發展及維護和平社會上，他們是有既得利益的同胞。他們也像一般人一樣，擁有家庭和朋友。警察是宣誓過要服務大眾的和事佬。

警察是我们的同胞

警察是当地社区的一部分。他们是我们的同胞，为了保护大家的生命安全和社会稳定而被赋予了特殊的使命。他们和我们一样，有家人，有朋友。警察是立誓保护公共安全的和平之子。

Authors, 關於作者，著者

Wayne L. Davis, Ph.D.

Wayne L. Davis holds a Bachelor of Science in Electrical Engineering, a Master of Science in Business Administration, and a Ph.D. in Criminal Justice. Dr. Davis has graduated from city, state, and federal law enforcement academies and he has over 20 years of law enforcement experience with city, state, and federal law enforcement agencies. Dr. Davis was a field training officer with the Indiana State Police and has received the U.S. Customs & Border Protection Commissioner's Award.

韋恩•戴維斯 博士

韋恩•戴維斯擁有電機工程學理學學士，企業管理理學碩士，和刑事司法博士學位。戴維斯博士畢業於城市級、州級，和聯邦級執法學院，而且他與上述機構共事超過二十年。戴維斯博士是訓練印第安那州州警察的專員，並且獲得美國海關邊防警長獎。

韦恩 L. 戴维斯博士

戴维斯博士拥有电子工程的学士学位，工商管理的硕士学位以及刑事司法学的博士学位。同时，戴维斯博士是一位经验丰富的执法者，他分别毕业于市、州以及联邦的警察学院，并服务于市级、州级和联邦的警务部门超过二十年。戴维斯博士曾担任印第安纳州警局的训练教官，并曾荣获美国海关&边防理事奖。

Yu-Wen Lai

Yu-Wen Lai holds a Bachelor of Arts in Chinese Literature from National Chengchi University in Taiwan. She teaches Chinese Language and continues her master's degree at Lincoln Memorial University.

賴郁雯

賴郁雯畢業於臺灣國立政治大學中國文學系，目前於美國林肯紀念大學擔任中文教師，以及攻讀碩士學位。

赖郁雯

赖郁雯毕业于台湾国立政治大学中文学系，目前于美国林肯纪念大学担任中文教师，以及攻读硕士学位。

Qiangjian Song

Qiangjian Song holds undergraduate degrees of theology and education administration. Currently, he is working on his master degree of Criminal Justice at Lincoln Memorial University.

宋強建

宋強建曾獲得神學和教育管理的本科學歷。目前於林肯紀念大學修讀刑事司法學碩士學位。

宋强建

宋强建曾获得神学和教育管理的本科学历。目前于林肯纪念大学修读刑事司法学硕士学位。

www.ingramcontent.com/pod-product-compliance
Lightning Source LLC
Chambersburg PA
CBHW050417290526
45786CB00003B/1304